AMERICAN HUMANE

Protecting Children & Animals Since 1877

Top 10 Dogs for Kids

Ann Graham Gaines

Enslow Elementary

an imprint of

Enslow Publishers, Inc.

40 Industrial Road
Box 398
Berkeley Heights, NJ 07922
USA

http://www.enslow.com

AMERICAN HUMANE

Protecting Children & Animals Since 1877

Founded in 1877, the American Humane Association is the oldest national organization dedicated to protecting both children and animals. Through a network of child and animal protection agencies and individuals, the American Humane Association develops policies, legislation, curricula, and training programs to protect children and animals from abuse, neglect, and exploitation. To learn how you can support the vision of a nation where no child or animal will ever be a victim of willful abuse or neglect, visit www.americanhumane.org, phone (303) 792-9900, or write to the American Humane Association at 63 Inverness Drive East, Englewood, Colorado, 80112-5117.

Enslow Elementary, an imprint of Enslow Publishers, Inc.

Enslow Elementary® is a registered trademark of Enslow Publishers, Inc.

Library of Congress Cataloging-in-Publication Data

Gaines, Ann.
   Top 10 dogs for kids / Ann Graham Gaines.
      p. cm. — (Top pets for kids with American Humane)
   Summary: "Provides facts on the top ten dog breeds for kids and how to care for them"—Provided by publisher.
   Includes bibliographical references and index.
   ISBN-13: 978-0-7660-3070-1
   ISBN-10: 0-7660-3070-9
   1. Dog breeds—Juvenile literature. 2. Dogs—Juvenile literature.
I. Title. II. Title: Top ten dogs for kids.
   SF426.5.G35 2008
   636.7—dc22   2007024510

Printed in the United States of America
102011 Lake Book Manufacturing, Inc., Melrose Park, IL

10 9 8 7 6 5

The top 10 dogs are approved by the American Humane Association and are listed alphabetically.

To Our Readers:
We have done our best to make sure that all Internet Addresses in this book were active and appropriate when we went to press. However, the author and publisher have no control over and assume no liability for the material available on those Internet sites or on other Web sites they may link to. Any comments or suggestions can be sent by e-mail to comments@enslow.com or to the address on the back cover.

♻ Enslow Publishers, Inc., is committed to printing our books on recycled paper. The paper in every book contains 10% to 30% post-consumer waste (PCW). The cover board on the outside of each book contains 100% PCW. Our goal is to do our part to help young people and the environment too!

Cover Photo: Ron Kimball/Ron Kimball Stock
Interior Photos: Alamy/mediacolor's, p. 4; Alamy/Arco Images, p. 8; Alamy/Royalty-Free/Corbis, p. 14; Alamy/Daniel Dempster Photography, p. 32; Equine Photography by Suzanne, p. 35; iStockphoto.com/Todd Taulman, p. 2; iStockphoto.com/Aric Vyhmeister, pp. 3, 26; iStockphoto.com/Denise McQuillen, pp. 5, 9, 17, 42; iStockphoto.com/Greg Nicholas, pp. 6, 7, 41; iStockphoto.com/Alexey Stiop, pp. 13, 15; iStockphoto.com/Ben Conlan, p. 23; iStockphoto.com/Justin Horrocks, p. 25; iStockphoto.com/Joop Snijder, p. 27; iStockphoto.com/Natalia Guseva, p. 28; iStockphoto.com/Serdar Yagci, p. 29; iStockphoto.com/Paul Erickson, p. 30; iStockphoto.com/Carl Durocher, p. 31; iStockphoto.com/Brenda A. Smith, p. 33; iStockphoto.com/Charles Humphries, p. 36; iStockphoto.com/Eric Isselée, p. 37; iStockphoto.com/Ken Hurst, p. 39; iStockphoto.com/Loretta Hostettler, p. 40; iStockphoto.com/Jill Fromer, p. 46; iStockphoto.com/walik, p. 47; iStockphoto.com/Tatiana Morozova, p. 48; Photo Researchers, Inc./Richard Hutchings, p. 20; Ron Kimball Stock/Renee Stockdale, pp. 1, 11, 12, 18; Ron Kimball Stock/Ron Kimball, pp. 16, 22, 24, 34, 38, 44.

Contents

So You Want to Get a Dog?

All over the world, dogs are very popular pets. Why? One reason is because they are often devoted and loyal. Dogs can also be a lot of fun to play with!

If you want a dog, first make sure that having a dog as a pet is a good idea for your family. There are lots of different ways you can find out what it is really like

◀ A pet dog can be an exercise buddy, a good listener, and a loyal companion. In other words, a friend!

to have a dog. Talk to a veterinarian (vet) or to other dog owners. You can also go to the library to find many good books about dogs that contain detailed information.

You also need to think about your own life. Here are some things to consider:

▶ A dog will be a great choice of pet for you if you want a companion—an animal who spends a lot of time with you.

▶ You will also be a good "dog person" if you like to be outdoors and exercise.

▶ Can your family afford a dog? In other words, do you have enough money for food, visits to the vet, and medicine?

▶ Think about the space you have. Some dogs can live in an apartment, but many need a yard and lots of room to run and play.

▶ Your family will also need to have free time. Your dog will need attention and care every day!

If you decide that a dog is the pet for you, it is important to understand that having a dog (or any pet) means having a lot of responsibility. If you choose a dog, you will have this responsibility for many years. (On average, dogs live anywhere from 7 to 14 years.) But it will be very rewarding, too. Your dog can become a great friend.

How to Have a Happy and Healthy Dog

You have decided to get a dog. What do you need to know now? What will it take to keep your dog healthy and happy?

Food

At least once a day, you will need to feed your dog dry or canned food. You should ask your vet for advice about what type of

The right food, plenty of fresh water, and a clean eating area—life is good!

food is best for your dog. Many vets do not recommend feeding any dog "people food" (food from your table). Dogs also need a constant supply of fresh water to drink. You will need to change it every day and make sure it is clean and cool.

Grooming

You can groom your dog at home by brushing his coat. Some dogs need to go to a professional groomer for an occasional haircut so their coat does not become matted (tangled into thick knots). Your dog will also need his claws trimmed and his teeth and ears cleaned regularly.

A Comfortable Place to Live

Before you bring your dog home, be sure to prepare a place for her to sleep that is warm, comfortable, and clean. If your dog

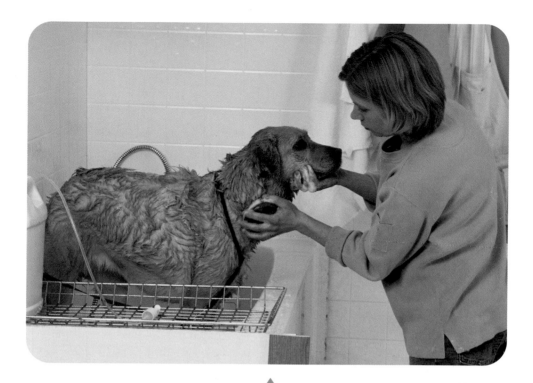

▲

A dog needs frequent baths to keep her coat healthy, beautiful and clean-smelling! A professional groomer can do this, or you can easily do it at home.

is going to spend time outside, make sure there is a fence that will not allow her to escape. A fence will help keep both your dog and other people safe. Your dog will also need shelter in your yard. This could be a dog house that you build with your family, or a ready-made one purchased at a pet supply store. All dog houses need to be in a location where there will never be too much sun and rain will not run in.

▲

A warm, comfortable, cozy place to sleep will ensure sweet dreams for your dog. You can buy a bed at a pet store, or make one yourself out of old, clean blankets or towels.

A Collar and Identification

Identification means a plastic or metal tag purchased at a vet's office or a pet supply store. On the tag, you will write—or a company will engrave— a phone number. It can be your number or your vet's. Either way, people will know who to call if your dog gets lost. Vets can also implant microchips in dogs, which make it easy to find out who owns them. It is like having a computerized name tag.

Exercise

Some dogs need a lot of exercise, such as running. Some need to go for walks more than once a day. And others just need a little exercise, such as playing with a ball inside the house. But all dogs need exercise!

▲

Your vet will be an important part of your dog's life. Be sure to bring your pet in for regular checkups. Have a list of questions for the vet each time you go.

Health Care

Your dog will need regular trips to the vet's office for shots and check-ups, and medical attention if he is sick or injured. The vet can also spay or neuter your dog. This means the doctor will perform an operation (spaying for female dogs, neutering for male dogs) that will make it impossible for your dog to produce puppies. This is good for your dog—it can mean a longer, healthier, happier life.

Positive Training

You can teach your dog how to act by rewarding good behavior. This is done by praising him or giving him a treat to eat. Positive training works much better than punishing a dog for doing something "bad." If you yell at him, he probably will not understand why. On the other hand, if you praise him for good behavior, instead of being afraid, the dog quickly learns that he will be rewarded for being obedient (behaving well).

Love and Affection

All dogs need their owners to pay attention to them, talk to them, and spend time with them. The great news is they can truly become another member of your family!

How to Choose the Right Dog

There are many, many different kinds of dogs. Which is the dog for you? There are a few questions to think about.

Large or Small?

If your family lives in an apartment, trailer, or other small space, you might want a small dog. Larger dogs usually need

◄ Bring the toys! Lively, active, playful dogs need lots of space to run around.

more space, so they might be a good choice if you live in the country or near a park where dogs are allowed.

Puppy or Adult?

Many people want puppies. After all, they are so cute! But sometimes it might be a better idea to get a dog who is already grown.

Puppies love to chew! Always have dog toys for yours to chew on. That way, she will be less likely to chew on things like shoes and furniture.

Why? First of all, there are many adult dogs who have been abandoned and now live at animal shelters. They need permanent homes. Also, adult dogs are generally calmer than puppies. Often they do not need a lot of training. They will not be as likely to chew on things they should not, bark every time someone comes to the door, or pee on the floor.

What Breed?

After you decide on a large or small dog and settle on whether or not to get a puppy, you can think more about what breed of dog is best for your family. Look at the breed descriptions in this book. Notice that some dogs need more exercise than others. Some dogs need extra attention. Some need extra grooming. To find out about other breeds, consult other books at

the library. You can also talk to your vet or ask for advice at an animal shelter.

Where Should I Get My Dog?

You are now ready to go find your pet. The best place to get a dog is at an animal shelter or rescue group. If you have your heart set on a specific breed, look for a breed rescue group or a breeder. Ask your vet for the name of a good breeder. It is not a good idea to get a dog from a pet shop or a friend, or to adopt a stray you find on the street.

Look for a dog who is friendly, attentive—who watches what is going on—and active. The dog should have clean, thick fur, bright eyes, a clean nose, and not be too thin or fat. All of these things are signs of good health.

An animal shelter is one of the best places to get a pet dog. But it can be hard to choose just one to bring home!

A beagle is a good choice for families with children.

Appearance

- Short coat in either two colors (mostly white with tan) or three colors (mostly white with black and light brown)
- Medium-sized body with muscular chest
- Curved tail tipped in white
- Domed head with square muzzle
- Long ears
- Brown eyes, sometimes described as sweet or pleading
- Height: about 18 inches
- Weight: 20 to 35 pounds

Chapter 1

Beagle

In the past, beagles were used by hunters to track rabbits and other small animals. They have an excellent sense of smell and are sometimes called scent hounds. Today the beagle is a very popular pet. This breed is a good choice for families with children.

General Behavior

Beagles:
1. are "merry" by nature, and like to play.
2. often bark or howl at the unfamiliar—like a delivery truck or a strange dog.
3. are generally obedient except when they have smelled something they want to go after.
4. are very intelligent.
5. have a lot of energy.

Special Needs

Beagles get bored easily, so they need a lot of attention.

◄ If you are looking for a smart, happy, playful friend to spend time with, a beagle may be the dog for you!

Boxers need lots of attention and exercise.

Appearance

- Short, shiny coat in fawn, red, or brindle (with streaks of black and tan)
- Sometimes have a white chest, belly, or feet. Some have a black "mask" on their face.
- Powerful, muscular body
- Upward-pointing, short tail
- Square head and flat face, with skin in folds around the jaw and wrinkles on the forehead
- Round, expressive eyes
- Height: about 25 inches
- Weight: up to 80 pounds

Chapter 2

Boxer

Boxers were once used as hunting dogs. Today they are considered a gentle breed. A boxer is a good match for you if you want a dog who has a lot of energy and will want to spend a lot of time with your family, or if you need a watchdog.

Special Needs

Boxers have more energy than many other dogs. They need lots of attention and exercise. Because of their very short coats, they also cannot stand extreme cold or heat.

Do you have lots of energy? Do you love to run, jump, and play? If so, you will love having a boxer for a pet!

General Behavior

Boxers:

1. are lively and like to run.
2. are playful and will jump, twist, and sometimes even somersault!
3. are very loyal and affectionate and will seek out members of the family.
4. will fight if they sense danger.
5. will not want to spend a lot of time alone, especially outside.
6. have great hearing and make good watchdogs.

Collies are eager to please and generally easy to train.

Appearance

- Rough collies have long, silky coats and a ruff (a ring of thick fur) around their necks. Smooth collies' coats are short and smooth.
- Long, thin but strong body
- Long tail, full in rough collie
- Pointed face
- Large ears that tend to stand straight up when the dog is excited
- Almond-shaped eyes, which are sometimes blue
- Height: up to 27 inches
- Weight: 50 to 70 pounds

Chapter 3

Collie

The most famous collie of all time was Lassie, the star of a 1950s television show. Lassie made the collie a very popular dog in the United States. There are two types of collies—rough and smooth.

General Behavior

Collies:

1. will try to protect family members from danger.
2. sometimes "herd" small children, trying to prevent them from wandering off.
3. love to be with people and will be glad to lie on your bed or sofa, if you let them.
4. are eager to please and generally easy to train.

Special Needs

Collies are very energetic and can get in trouble if they are left alone a lot or are not given enough exercise.

◀ If you want an energetic but snuggly companion who will protect you, get a collie!

German shepherds make great search-and-rescue dogs.

Appearance

- Short hair (commonly black and tan)
- Powerful, sturdy body, often compared to a wolf's body
- Bushy tail
- Wide head
- Pointed ears
- Almond-shaped dark eyes
- Height: about 24 inches
- Weight: up to 95 pounds

German Shepherd

German shepherds make great working dogs. They are often used by police forces and the military, and as service dogs for the disabled. They are best for families with a lot of time to exercise a dog. Despite their larger size, they can even live in an apartment if you are able to take them out every day.

General Behavior

German shepherds:

1. are loyal and dedicated and are good at guarding a home and family.
2. do not need constant companionship—they can be content spending some time by themselves.
3. may be fearless, but are not usually aggressive.
4. enjoy long walks and playing hard.
5. are easily trained.

Special Needs

German shepherds are generally easy to get along with. They are happiest, however, when they have a job or are being trained. That is why they make great guide dogs or search-and-rescue dogs.

◄ A German shepherd is strong and independent, and will always stand by you. Take one home!

Golden retrievers are athletic, and love to run and swim.

Appearance

- Thick, sometimes wavy golden coat
- Tall body, long legs, thick tail
- Broad, slightly rounded head
- Soft, floppy ears
- Deep brown eyes
- Height: up to 24 inches
- Weight: about 65 pounds

Chapter 5

Golden Retriever

Golden retrievers were bred by Scottish hunters to retrieve the birds they shot. This will be a good breed for your family if there are children in the household, and if you would like a constant companion.

Special Needs

Golden retrievers usually need a lot of attention. They also need a lot of exercise. To keep their coat healthy and looking great, they need to be brushed three or four times a week, more than many other dogs.

If you are looking for an outgoing, loving friend who likes to be around kids, a golden retriever may be the dog for you!

General Behavior

Golden retrievers:

1. are athletic, and love to run and swim.
2. are usually so friendly that they do not make very good guard dogs—they tend to greet strangers not by barking, but with a wagging tail!
3. are affectionate and gentlc and likc to be with their family.
4. are obedient, which makes them easy to handle despite their size.
5. are very outgoing and socialize easily with other dogs and humans.

Labrador retrievers love water and are great swimmers.

Labrador Retriever

Labrador retrievers were originally bred to help fishermen. The dogs would swim out to pull fishing nets to shore. A "Lab" will be a great choice for you if you really like to exercise and will enjoy having a dog who wants to run and play outside.

General Behavior

Labrador retrievers:

1. are strong and athletic and can run and swim for hours.
2. are friendly and get along not just with humans, but other dogs, too.
3. can be mischievous and will get into trouble by digging, for example, if left alone too long.
4. are sweet-tempered and play well with kids.

Special Needs

Labrador retrievers love water. Most want to swim and will sometimes do so even if their owners do not want them to!

◄ Do you like adventure? Do you like to swim and make new friends? If so, a Labrador retriever may be the perfect pet!

Mixed breeds are an excellent choice for people who want a unique dog.

Appearance

Short hair, long hair, silky hair, coarse hair—mixed-breed dogs can have any type! They also come in all shapes and sizes, and many colors—from white to yellow to brown to tan to red to black.

Chapter 7

Mixed Breed

Purebred dogs come from parents who are both of the same breed. Many dogs are not purebreds, but mixed breeds. In other words, they are a mix of more than one type of dog. Mixed breeds are a great choice for people who want a one-of-a-kind dog. Another reason they can be a good choice is because they are often easy-going.

General Behavior

Mixed breeds:

1. can be very trainable.
2. make excellent companions because they tend to be friendly.
3. often live longer and healthier lives than many purebreds. They do not have the health problems caused by some breeding practices, which can cause genetic disorders.

Special Needs

Since mixed-breed dogs often come from shelters or rescue groups, many could use extra love!

◄ Are you looking for a unique, easy-going companion to hang out with? If so, a mixed breed may be the dog for you.

Pugs are friendly and will sit in your lap.

Appearance

- Short, smooth hair in silver, fawn (a very light tan), apricot (light orange), or black, with black muzzle and ears
- Small, square body
- Round face, with lots of wrinkles
- Large, deep-set, expressive eyes
- Small ears, sometimes described as "buttons"
- Curled tail
- Height: 10 or 11 inches
- Weight: about 15 pounds

Pug

Pugs were first raised in China. They make good pets for families that want a constant companion.

General Behavior

Pugs:

1. can be lively and playful, but also like to sleep a lot.
2. might learn to do tricks, such as somersaults.
3. are sometimes stubborn and may not always want to obey.
4. are friendly and will sit in your lap.
5. are very patient.

Special Needs

Pugs can easily become overweight. They may be able to live in a small home, but they need lots of exercise. They can get overheated, so you need to make sure they stay cool.

◀ Are you looking for a cuddly, patient companion who would love to learn some tricks? If so, a pug may be the dog for you!

Shih tzus are ideal dogs for people who live in the city.

Appearance

- Long, luxurious hair that will reach the ground
- A wide range of colors. The most common are white, gold, tan, and brown.
- Compact, sturdy body
- Round head and flat face with a short snout
- Long ears
- Wide-spread, round eyes
- Height: 8 to 11 inches
- Weight: 9 to 16 pounds

Chapter 9

Shih Tzu

The shih tzu (SHEED-zoo) was first bred for the emperor of China as a guard dog (the dogs were trained to bark if they sensed danger). The breed came to the United States in the 1930s. It is a good match for you if you want a dog who will always want to play and will be as happy playing inside as going for a walk. These are ideal dogs for people who live in the city.

General Behavior

Shih tzus:
1. have been described as "spunky."
2. love to play and romp.
3. are affectionate and like to be petted and held.
4. can be stubborn and hard to train.

Special Needs

Shih tzus must be brushed every day and need to have their fur trimmed often. It gets tangled if it grows too long, and can even interfere with walking. Their eyes also need to be cleaned daily. They need to be kept inside since they cannot stand much heat.

◄ Do you live in a small home or apartment? If so, consider a shih tzu—a playful, cuddly friend with real attitude!

Standard poodles tend to show off!

Appearance

- Thick, curly coat of hair in a wide range of colors, including white, cream, tan, "blue," gray, or black
- Tall, thin body with broad chest and long legs
- Long, thin face
- Oval, very dark eyes
- Wide ears that hang down close to the head
- Height: 21 to 27 inches
- Weight: 45 to 65 pounds

Chapter 10

Standard Poodle

Standard poodles are the largest of the three types of poodles (the others are toy and miniature). They make great pets for families that want a constant companion. A poodle's fur does not shed, so it is the perfect pet for people with allergies. Some owners have their poodles' fur clipped into fancy patterns.

General Behavior

Standard poodles:

1. are very intelligent.
2. tend to show off.
3. often like to swim.
4. are eager to please.
5. can live in an apartment, but like most dogs, need a lot of exercise.

Special Needs

Standard poodles often become very attached to people, and do not like to be left alone. They also need more grooming than most other breeds of dog.

How about a dog who has lots of energy, loves to entertain, and is eager to please? That is a standard poodle!

Getting to Know Your Dog

It is time to bring your new dog home—let the fun begin!

The first thing you need to do is introduce your dog to the other members of your family. Talk to your younger brothers and sisters about how to treat your dog. One of the most important things for them to understand is that dogs generally do not like a lot of noise. They do not want to have their ears pulled or tail tugged.

You will have to warn them that dogs can bite, especially if they are hurt or afraid.

Other Dogs

If you already have another dog, get a friend or family member to help you introduce the dogs to one another. It is best not to do this in your house. Go to a nearby park or a friend's yard. That way, the dog who has already been living with you is less likely to see the newcomer as a threat.

Feeding and Care

Make sure you have a clear plan for feeding and taking care of your dog. If more than one person will be responsible for your pet, it might help to make a schedule. Include feeding, watering, exercising, and grooming in your schedule.

▲

Not all pets will get along with each other at first. It can take lots of time and patience to introduce them to one another.

Checkup

Within just one or two days of getting your dog, you need to take her to a vet for a checkup. This is a good time to ask about the signs of a healthy dog. The vet may talk about bright eyes, a wet nose, and a clean coat. Also ask the vet about any health problems your breed tends to have.

Training

Puppies need house training to avoid indoor "accidents." Older dogs may need some training, too, to learn not to jump on people or furniture, or bark too much. When training a dog, remember to use a positive approach. Reward good behavior with a treat, and never, ever hit your dog for any reason.

Plenty of Love

When you bring your new pet home, the most important thing of all is to have lots of patience, and to give him plenty of love and affection. Having a dog means taking on a great deal of responsibility. But this responsibility can be very rewarding.

Glossary

animal shelter—A place where people can adopt animals that other people can no longer care for.

breeder—A person who breeds a certain type of dog.

groomer—A person who bathes, brushes, and clips (trims the hair of) dogs for a living.

matted—Tangled into thick knots.

microchip—A tiny computer chip that is embedded under a dog's skin. It holds identification information about the dog. It can be scanned by a veterinarian to read the information.

muzzle—The snout, or the area of the face that includes a dog's mouth and jaw.

neutered—When male dogs have the organs removed that help them produce puppies.

obedient—Well-behaved.

purebred—A dog whose parents are of the same breed.

spayed—When female dogs have the organs removed that help them produce puppies.

veterinarian (vet)—A doctor who takes care of animals.

Further Reading

Adelman, Beth. *Good Dog! Dog Care for Kids.* Chanhassen, Minn.: Child's World, 2007.

Kehret, Peg. *Shelter Dogs: Amazing Stories of Adopted Strays.* Morton Grove, Ill.: Albert Whitman, 2003.

Mehus-Roe, Kristin. *Dogs for Kids!* Irvine, Cal.: BowTie Press, 2007.

Whitehead, Sarah. *How to Speak Dog.* New York: Scholastic Reference, 2008.

Internet Addresses

American Humane Association
http://www.americanhumane.org

American Kennel Club
http://www.akc.org/

Woof! (from the PBS program)
http://www.pbs.org/wgbh/woof/index.html

Index